My Scrap Book

Place a photograph of you
in this space.
Trim the photograph to fit.

This book is devoted
to the special memories and stories of

Princess ______________________________

Snow White, Cinderella, Aurora,
Jasmine, Belle and Ariel
all help share this most
fascinating story
of a true Princess.

My Family

Place a photograph of your
family in this space.
Trim the photograph to fit.

Place a photograph of your
family in this space.
Trim the photograph to fit.

Place a photograph of your
family in this space.
Trim the photograph to fit.

Aurora was named after the dawn,
for she filled her family's lives with sunshine.

My Family

My name is Mala Mala ____________________

and I was born on the ______ day of ____________________

in the year ____________

I live with ____

____

and our address is ______________________________________

____

To protect Aurora from the evil villian Maleficent, the three good fairies, Fauna, Flora and Merryweather, took the Princess to a secret hiding place.

About Me

My very own fairy tale began when ______________________

____

____

____

____

____

____

If the girl can be found whom the slipper fits, that girl shall be the princess bride.

About Me

My eyes are

- [ ] Blue
- [ ] Brown
- [ ] Green
- [ ] Hazel

My hair is

- [ ] Blonde
- [ ] Brown
- [ ] Red
- [ ] Black

My hair is

- [ ] Straight
- [ ] Curly
- [ ] Wavy

Cinderella revealed the matching slipper
and placed it on her dainty foot – a perfect fit!

My Friends

Name	Address

Hearing the birds sweet melody, *Snow White* looked up and smiled,
her woodland friends crept closer, snuggling in her lap or nestling in her arms.

My Friends

I first met my friend, ____________________________________
insert name of friend

when ____

____

____

____

____

____

____

Following the birds, deer and squirrels Snow White came upon a tiny cottage nestling in a clearing.

choose a theme for
this page and decorate

Rajah the pet tiger listens intently as *Jasmine* shares her secret plan
– to leave the palace and experience life in the real world.

choose a theme for
this page and decorate

School

School name ______________________________

My teachers ______________ ______________

______________ ______________

______________ ______________

______________ ______________

The class I enjoy most is ______________________

Even though the Beast would not allow Belle to leave his castle, knowing about her love of books he encouraged her to explore his vast library.

Achievements

Things I Like

In my free time I like to:

- [ ] Cook
- [ ] Play Sport
- [ ] Play Music
- [ ] Garden
- [ ] Other ______________________
- [ ] Sew
- [ ] Read
- [ ] Paint/draw
- [ ] Shop

Ariel loved nothing more than singing whilst swimming throughout her beautiful aquatic home... that is until she met Prince Eric!

Things I Like

I like

because

Suddenly the ability to walk was a skill that Ariel desperately wanted to acquire.

Celebrations

A moonlit night, filled with romance and adventure.
Is it music or is my heart singing?

Celebrations

Remember…Never stop dreaming or dancing!

Here is where we leave this enchanting tale of

Princess ______________________

When you believe in your dreams,
magic will await wherever you go.

The treasured photographs and keepsakes
contained within will always remind you
of the special journey you have begun.

Snow White, Cinderella, Aurora,
Jasmine, Belle and Ariel

feel cherished to share
in your memories.